LEARNING
LIFE

LEARNING
LIFE

ROGER WALTER

Pacific Press®
Publishing Association
Nampa, Idaho | www.pacificpress.com

Cover design by David Berthiaume
Cover design resources from GettyImages.com
Interior design by Aaron Troia

The author assumes full responsibility for the accuracy of all facts and quotations as cited in this book.

To order additional copies of this book, call toll-free 1-800-765-6955, or visit AdventistBookCenter.com.

ISBN 978-0-8163-6936-2

September 2023

DEDICATION

This book is dedicated to my partner in life, Gail, who battled through this with me as we found our way into a personal spiritual life that really does make a difference.

It is also dedicated to those who have taken up the journey with us: my wonderful kids, people at The Adventure in Colorado, and at the Adventist Community Church in Vancouver, Washington, as well as everywhere else it has spread.

Keep on the journey; it's the most important thing you will ever do.

CONTENTS

Acknowledgments   9

Introduction   11

Chapter One: Anger Issues   15

Chapter Two: A New Journey   26

Chapter Three: YOU GOT A PROBLEM?   37

Chapter Four: Discovering the Unknown Piece   48

Chapter Five: Struggles   59

Chapter Six: Over Time   71

Chapter Seven: Same Old, Same Old   79

Chapter Eight: The Good-Enough Continuum   97

Chapter Nine: Daniel   109

Chapter Ten: As Easy as a Workout   116

ACKNOWLEDGMENTS

First, I want to thank God for the life change He has worked in me along this journey. I want to thank my wife, Gail, who has been on this devotional journey with me from the get-go. I want to thank her for asking me every morning, "What did you read about today?" Which together we found to be the final piece of the puzzle that makes it stick in our lives. I would also like to thank my daughter Krista for the work she did on an earlier version of this book. Your time, Krista, was invaluable, motivating me to finally follow through with getting this written, and to think through what needed to be said correctly. I want to say thank you to my children for listening to me talk about and ask the same questions of you each morning at breakfast. Finally, I want to thank Wayne Cordeiro and Dwight Nelson, without whom this journey would have never started.

INTRODUCTION

The book you hold in your hands is, in essence, a story of my spiritual life. As you read it, please do not accuse me with a judgmental attitude about the things I have done wrong. Rather, judge me on the growth and the journey I have been on since I was baptized and became a Christian.

I believe this is the most important journey any of us will ever take, and it is one that the devil will attack with his greatest vengeance. Why? Because the journey you will read about and hopefully choose for your own life will have the biggest impact on keeping you in your relationship with the Lord. The devil does not want that, and thus, his attacks will follow.

However, the path will lead you down the road of righteousness by faith, and the rewards of this journey are truly out of this world.

What fruit were you getting at that time from the things of which you are now ashamed? For the end of those things is death. But now that you have been set free from sin and have become slaves of God, the fruit you get leads to sanctification and its end, eternal life. For the wages of sin is death, but the free gift of God is eternal life in Christ Jesus our Lord (Romans 6:21–23).

Years ago, I came across what has become my life verse. This next passage defines what I'm trying to express in this book more than anything. I simply want to help people find the path that will help them add to their faith.

His divine power has granted to us all things that pertain to life and godliness, through the knowledge of him who called us to his own glory and excellence, by which he has granted to us his precious and very great promises, so that through them you may become partakers of the divine nature, having escaped from the corruption that is in the world because of sinful desire. For this very reason, make every effort to supplement your faith with virtue, and virtue with knowledge, and knowledge with self-control, and self-control with steadfastness, and steadfastness with godliness, and godliness with brotherly affection, and brotherly affection with love. For if these qualities are yours and are increasing, they keep you from being ineffective or unfruitful in the knowledge of our Lord Jesus Christ. For whoever lacks these qualities is so nearsighted that he is blind, having forgotten that he was cleansed from his former sins. Therefore, brothers, be all the more diligent to confirm your calling and election, for if you practice these qualities you will never fall. For in this way there will be richly provided for you an entrance into the eternal kingdom of our Lord and Savior Jesus Christ (2 Peter 1:3–11).

My prayer as you read this book is that you will be entertained and maybe laugh, and yet I hope that the points I make will change your life forever. Truly.

* * * * *

You will read more about a handy resource called the *Life Journal* as we go forward. You may order it and other Life resources from liferesources.cc. Used by permission.

ONE

ANGER ISSUES

Ever had one of those days that seemed to go so well until one little thing took over and destroyed the whole day for you? Yeah, we probably all have. My wife, Gail, and I were on a bike ride one day many years ago. We were still newlyweds and still blissfully thinking this world was marvelous. The sky was blue, the grass was green, and life was wonderful. About ten miles into the ride, we needed to stop, drink some water and eat some food. We pulled into a small parking lot beside what looked like an apartment building. We found a grassy spot near the road where we could sit, stretch our legs, and get ready to start the remaining ten miles home.

After about ten minutes, we grabbed our bikes and prepared to head for home. Gail got on her bike first and began riding toward the parking lot exit. I was a few seconds behind. In those very few short moments, a car drove up beside my wife, and two people, an elderly man and woman, rolled down their window and began yelling at her!

Now, if you want to get me fired-up mad, just go after someone I love.

As it turns out, this was a private residential community, and the parking lot was off-limits to non-residents. However, we had not seen any signs when we rode up and stopped. And it could hardly be considered that we were even in the parking lot. Of course, at that moment, no sign would have made any difference whatsoever. I had no idea, nor could I see any logical reason, why they would be yelling at my sweet wife. I stepped up into high gear and came up to them, skidding both tires between Gail and the car. As I deftly slid into position, I leaned down near their window and face-to-face with the screaming lady, and in a very (ahem) Christian-like, pastoral manner, screamed back, "YOU GOT A PROBLEM?"

This only escalated the confrontation. About two minutes later, they sped off in a huff, and we rode away. After getting over her initial shock, my wife went back to enjoying the bike ride—checking out the scenery, noting the flowers, and getting her exercise. Me, on the other hand—well, it ruined the rest of my day. I could not stop fuming and ranting. I rode pretty hard on the way back home, mumbling to myself about what I should have said and being exasperated about what had been said. The nerve of those people!

I was still grumbling about it that evening when I

Somehow, I missed *what I was doing wrong*. All I knew was you better not attack someone I love, or my wrath would come out pretty hard. It honestly never even crossed my mind that yelling and escalating the issue was just as wrong. I thought it was the right thing to do. It turns out I was dead wrong. I was making a small issue large.

went to the church to lead a meeting where my topic was God's grace and forgiveness! I grumbled about it all the way home after the meeting. (Clearly, something had not clicked with me about the grace-and-forgiveness talk I had just given.) As I write these words today, I realize that I have told that story countless times in sermons, to friends, and to myself to show how awful those people were and what they had done wrong. Somehow, I missed *what I was doing wrong.* All I knew was you better not attack someone I love, or my wrath would come out pretty hard. It honestly never even crossed my mind that yelling and escalating the issue was just as wrong. I thought it was the right thing to do. It turns out I was dead wrong. I was making a small issue large.

My problem was anger. Anger is an interesting thing. It can take over. Even when your rational mind is saying, "Do not go there," your lips, voice, and face take over, and the anger spills out. For some of us, that anger comes out too often and too easily. In my case, the anger came way too easily for me.

It troubled me. I had been a Christian since I was twelve. I was now about twenty-five. Why wasn't it making any difference in my anger issues? Why wasn't it changing me? I wondered at times why my anger was so explosive, and I thought about how that wasn't really reflecting Christ. And, of course, I certainly didn't want my church members to ever notice this character trait.

The book of James talks about anger in very clear terms: "My dear brothers and sisters, take note of this:

Everyone should be quick to listen, slow to speak and slow to become angry, because human anger does not produce the righteousness that God desires" (James 1:19, 20, NIV).

If we are slow to speak and quick to listen, it will make us also slow to anger. That's good because, as James says, it does not produce anything we really want out of life. David, in Psalms, says the same thing: "Refrain from anger and turn from wrath; do not fret—it leads only to evil" (Psalm 37:8, NIV).

There are more writers of Scripture that have something to say about what anger does to you:

> "Be angry and do not sin; do not let the sun go down on your anger" (Ephesians 4:26).

> "Be not quick in your spirit to become angry, for anger lodges in the heart of fools" (Ecclesiastes 7:9).

> "A man of wrath stirs up strife, and one given to anger causes much transgression" (Proverbs 29:22).

Jump ahead with me about three years after our bicycling incident. Gail and I were going down to Coquille, Oregon, to look for housing. It seemed pretty obvious that the denomination was going to transfer us there, and we wanted to get a jump-start on the move by looking for housing.* On the way back from our fruitless house-hunting trip, we stopped at the only place along the way to get something to eat. Dairy Queen. Now, DQ is not noted for fine dining. But we were hungry, and anything would do. We were not in the mood for ice cream; we were hungry. As our luck would have it, they offered a bean burrito. I ordered two, along with something cold to drink. When the order was complete, I happily grabbed the bag and whistled as I headed to the car with visions of savory bean burritos in my head. Ah!

We were about two miles away when after Gail's first bite, she said in disgust, "This is not a bean burrito." Now, to be sure, I was thinking that she was wrong. This is Dairy Queen. It's a national chain. They do not make mistakes. I took a bite of mine to show her that she was clearly wrong, and as I chewed, we meandered down the road further. Gail relented and took a second bite, and said just as adamantly as the first time, "This is meat!" She handed it to me to look at, and sure enough, there was a hunk of meat, big enough to choke a horsefly. It was unmistakable as it sat on top of the burrito.

I reluctantly turned around. It took a while on the winding backwoods highway. Honestly, if it had been my burrito, I probably would have just swallowed and moved on. I was not raised as a vegetarian and therefore was not repulsed by the thought of eating something that formerly had a face. Gail, on the other hand, had only

---

* We never did move there, but that is another story.

tasted meat once and was profoundly disgusted by it. She had no intention of eating a meat burrito. She also has a strong sense of justice that prevented us from exchanging burritos. She was prepared to just stay hungry and did not want me to turn around. Even though I knew she would not eat mine, she was as hungry as I was.

I should have known better. I should have known I was not good with confrontation. I should have known that this backwater Dairy Queen which looked like a local greasy spoon, was not going to like some vegetarian complaining about a little meat. However, I was clueless that day. I should have listened to Psalm 37:8 and realized that complaining would lead only to greater problems. But I did not think of that at the time. I drove to the DQ and into the same parking spot, got out and walked calmly up to the ordering window, and said as politely as I could that the order we had received was incorrect.

The lady looked at me with mild disdain as if to say, "Your order wasn't wrong; I made it myself." Instead, she asked rather coolly, "How was it wrong?" I politely told her about the issue, and all she said was, "That's a bean burrito." I held up the burrito with the little quarter pounder perched on top so she could view it through the glass. She was obviously mistaken. "Please look. This is not a bean here."

At this point, the veins in her neck began to bulge, and she became irate and yelled, "I said it is a bean burrito!" Honestly, I was a bit surprised by this reaction. I mean, I was being nice up to this point. But I do not like getting

21

yelled at, and I did not respond very well. I reached into the burrito and held up that nasty little piece of flesh and held it straight up for her to see. Yet, she never took her eyes off of mine, thereby avoiding any eye contact with that little bit of cow. She yelled again, "IT'S A BEAN BURRITO!" Then she shut the little sliding window between us and stared at me.

Here's where I got very "pastoral" with her. I nearly pulled the window out of its slider as I (ahem) "calmly" but rapidly slid it way past the usual open stopping point. I thrust my face through the window, held the burrito under her nose, and just as calmly screamed back at her through my spittle, "THIS IS NOT A BEAN! IT IS NOT A BEAN BURRITO! TAKE A LOOK, AT LEAST!"

She took the burrito from my hands, but she never took her eyes off of me, therefore never laying eyes on the hunk of wilting flesh resting on top of the burrito. She screamed back at me, "IT'S A BEAN! IT'S A BEAN!" Then she shut her window again and turned and stomped into the back-room office and slammed the door on me. Conversation over.

I was dumbfounded. Not only had a calm discussion turned into a screaming match, but now I did not even have the burrito that I paid for. I finally acknowledged defeat and went back to the car. I griped and complained the rest of the way home. My poor wife was so embarrassed that I would even ask for an exchange of the order in the first place, and then to see *that* happen—wow! It ruined my whole day. I vowed I would never eat at a

Dairy Queen again. I actually looked up the address of that store and wrote them a letter of complaint—and that was before Google when it still took a bit of time and effort to find the address. I never heard back. I have since forgiven Dairy Queen but have never been back to that particular location.

As you may be able to tell, there were some rather glaring un-Christian-like issues hiding deep in my life. Anger, not one of the better virtues, seemed to boil over in my life. Where did it come from, and how should I deal with it? Those are big questions that are not often solved by years on a counselor's couch. Yet, when I was honest with myself, I knew it needed to be dealt with. No one would say that screaming about a burrito is in any way Christlike or Christian. My anger was going to destroy me if I did not get a handle on it.

Where am I going with these stories? I tell you about them simply to show that I had some deep-seated anger issues that, in the seventeen years since I had become a Christian, had never gone away. To say that my Christian experience was small is to state the obvious. Yet, I was a pastor seeking to lead others into a deeper spiritual experience.

What I want to address in this book is that there is a way to make Christianity work. It is a method that deals with your own personal issues, allowing God to take them up and fight the battles for you. And I can testify that it works for me! I am excited to tell you that although my anger issues are not completely gone, I have taken

There is a way to make
Christianity work. It is a
method that deals with
your own personal issues,
allowing God to take them
up and fight the battles
for you. And I can testify
it works for me!

incredible leaps forward toward a more positive attitude, and I believe the anger will all go away. I have become convinced that I will someday die with a smile on my face because a smile has become my usual expression and my common response.

When I say I expect to die with a smile on my face, I am not saying I will die while doing something incredibly fun that is making me smile. I am simply saying that when I die, I want to have a smile permanently etched on my face. I want my default aging look to be a smile. Many people default to a frown as they age. It is a product of gravity. The idea of defaulting to a smile has motivated me to embark on a journey of understanding and applying tenderness, humility, and compassion to my life. I read quotes and promises reminding me to stay on this journey daily. As I begin each day going over my prayer list, I am reminded to keep smiling, be tenderhearted, and stay humble. Powerful quotes lead me to become a more spirit-led Christian.

How does this happen? Read on. This book describes a story of personal spiritual growth that needs to be told over and over again. It is a story of the journey that has changed my life forever and helped me love the God of Scripture like I never have before. It is the story of tackling my anger issues head-on and seeing God win. I believe it's a story worth telling because not only have I seen my life changed, I've seen the change in hundreds of others on this same spiritual journey.

TWO

A NEW JOURNEY

Obviously, after reading the last chapter, you understand that I had a very explosive anger issue. I could blame it on my parents, but it was not their fault. I could blame it on other people, but my response is not their fault. I could blame my anger on being "hangry," eating too much, not getting enough sleep, losing work, or whatever. But making excuses would not solve anything. I simply had an issue that needed to be dealt with. I knew it, yet I did not know how to deal with it. But, even though I did not know how, God began doing something in my world that would shape me for the rest of my life.

In the summer of 1989, Pastor Dwight Nelson was the main speaker at a traditional church camp meeting in Gladstone, Oregon. As a pastor, my assignment was to work in the Earliteen* Division, so I was unable to hear him speak. Fortunately, the denominational leadership knew many of us wanted to listen to him, and gave us a set of recordings of his messages.

A few weeks after the camp meeting, Gail and I headed back east to visit her family. On the trip, we decided to listen to Pastor Nelson's messages. We drove a little blue Datsun 510 station wagon. We made a bed in the back so that while one of us was driving, the other could be sleeping. Don't try this at home, children; this was before seat-belt laws were in effect. Just before we arrived in Michigan to visit Gail's family, we listened to Pastor Nelson's very last message of the camp meeting series. In it, he outlined how he teaches people to have personal devotions. It basically had two components: read the Bible and journal your prayers.

In that last message, Pastor Nelson said two things that were unforgettable. First, when journaling your prayers, it is harder to lose track of what you are saying, and you end up praying longer. Second, do your devotions in the same place every day so you do not get distracted by the surroundings. Both of these suggestions made very good sense to me.

I had journaled my prayers before, but never in conjunction with a systematic reading plan. And never had I taken a passage of Scripture and prayed through what I saw the verse saying to me. In other words, I

---

* Earliteens are approximately ages 12–15.

First, when journaling your

prayers, it is harder to lose track

of what you are saying, and

you end up praying longer.

Second, do your devotions in

the same place every day so

you do not get distracted by the

surroundings.

had journaled my prayers, yes, but not the application of Scripture.

I had been a Christian for about fifteen years at that point in time. Prior to that, I had always wanted to have a personal devotional life. I had heard countless pastors preach about the need for one. I had heard numerous pastors say, "You need to study your Bible." "You need to read the Bible." And I always asked when I heard this, "How? I just want someone to show me how!" Everyone said, "Do it." No one said how.

I remember in college, a friend and fellow theology major and I were talking. It became apparent to both of us that we really did not know God personally. We had good morals. We were not sleeping around; we did not steal, swear, drink, etc. However, we were not spiritually minded. We were basically therapeutic moral deists. In other words, we believed in God and tried our best to live good moral lives, but we were not seeing God work in the day-to-day experience.

Christians produce a plethora of books about prayer, why it's good, and the blessings we will receive. Yet, again, my constant plea was, "I know I need to have personal devotions—to read and pray—but *how* do you do it?" Pastor Dwight Nelson had answers. He had provided the tools I needed.

Pastor Nelson made several suggestions: Start with the book of Mark. Read a chapter, or if that's too much, begin with a paragraph at a time. But one thing he said was not so much of a suggestion but a clear how-to—"Do it in the same place every day, so you don't get distracted by your surroundings." The problem at the time I heard this was that we were just arriving in Michigan for a six-day visit, and my surroundings would be very distracting—different home, different living room, different sights, different sounds. And my mother-in-law would want help with her computer issues—usually whenever it appeared that I was "not doing anything" except reading or praying. With that in mind, I made the decision that I would begin my new devotional plan, using the new tools, as soon as I was back home, in approximately a week.

You all know how good intentions go, right? We all get excited from seminars, sermons, and special events and make determined decisions. Yet, they almost never come to pass. But this time was different for me. I knew my Christian life lacked something significant. I was a pastor. I was supposed to be teaching others how to grow with Jesus, but I was not doing it myself. My devotional life was more off than on. So this time, I felt very motivated, and my decision was pretty rock-solid. Nevertheless, I was a tad worried because my past record showed a weak follow-through on my personal devotions.

When I was in seminary, I purchased a brand-new Bible with one-inch-wide margins. I decided to read one chapter in the book of Proverbs each day. I thought, *Why not utilize those wide margins and write my own thoughts and even prayers in the margins?* There was a lot of room. There are thirty-one chapters in Proverbs, and most months have thirty-one days. What a great idea! On the first day,

I read the first chapter in Proverbs and wrote some cool thoughts in the margins, and prayed. It was amazing! I loved it. The next day was really good too. The third day of this ritual began as usual, and I was looking forward to it. But, when I finished, it felt kind of ho-hum. The fourth day never happened. I still have that Bible and can still read those three days of thoughts. It fascinates me.

This was the pattern of my devotional life. Three days on, full of excitement, and thirty days off, with nothing devotional or prayer-like except the blessing at meals. My devotional life was more off than on. This caused a crisis for me. How in the world could I continue to pastor if I did not really have a relationship with Jesus myself? Was prayer really anything more than meal-time blessings and "now I lay me down to sleep?"

I tried a number of things—studying the Sabbath School lesson, studying a series of Bible studies, just reading the Bible, proof-texting my way through a subject, and a host of other ideas. None of them stuck for longer than a week.

So, when that recorded camp meeting message spoke, it spoke to my very core. I knew I needed this, and I knew I needed it immediately. But I delayed following the plan that the speaker had outlined. Despite this, however, for the first time in my life, I followed through on a decision that I had delayed for a week—as soon as we returned home, my wife and I both began devotions the way Pastor Nelson taught.

As I mentioned in the previous chapter, we loved to

bike-ride. At that point in my life, I was training to do triathlons. A triathlon is a combined swim, bike, and run. Each day, I kept a log of what training I had done, what my heart rate was, how far I had run, biked, or swam, and what my time and distances were. I was motivated to keep track so that I would really be prepared for the next race.

When we got home from Michigan, remembering the leadership proverb, "What gets measured, gets done," I added a column on my exercise log for personal devotions. I simply made a check mark to identify the days I had them. This was not some dogmatic, legalistic, record-keeping kind of mentality but rather a pure desire to motivate myself to further the work of God in me.

On my desk, I placed a picture of a man hitting a baseball with a bat that had this scripture attached to it: "For physical training is of some value, but godliness has value for all things, holding promise for both the present life and the life to come" (1 Timothy 4:8, NIV). This time I was motivated, and I did everything I could to keep myself motivated.

As I stated earlier, my devotional life was more off than on. Three days on, three weeks off. Two days on, two months off. In other words, even though I was trying to teach others from the Bible, I was not letting it teach me. However, I now began seeing something significant happening. I began applying Scripture in prayer to my own life, and I began to be challenged by what I saw. I went thirty days without missing a single day of devotions. I was shocked!

This was the pattern of my
devotional life. Three days
on, full of excitement, and
thirty days off, with nothing
devotional or prayer-like
except the blessing at
meals. My devotional life
was more off than on.

On the thirty-third day, something happened. I got exceptionally busy, I relaxed, or whatever, but I missed that day. It completely freaked me out! I had seen something exceptionally good happening in me as my life was being challenged and changed by daily time with God. I was afraid it would go away. I got up extra early the next day and went another thirty days without missing a day.

Thus began a new journey for me. My devotional life had flip-flopped. It was more on than off. I was clearly seeing a change, and I was excited about it. I was, for the first time in my life, seeing Scripture resonate with me in a way that was visibly life-changing. It was exciting to fall in love with Scripture again and to fall in love with God.

Pastor Nelson taught us not to get overwhelmed by what we read. He very clearly said to get a modern translation that is divided up into paragraphs and simply read a paragraph each day, then pray about what you have read. The prayers went like this:

"For God so loved the world, that He gave His only begotten Son . . ."

"Thank You, Lord, for giving me Your son. I am part of the world and am so glad that You have given me the Son. Your son, Jesus, has drastically changed the trajectory of my life. When I stop and think about where my life was headed and who I hung out with before I knew Jesus, I am overwhelmed by the gift of Your Son to me. Thank You."

The first day I did this, my devotions lasted an hour. I had just spent an hour praying and reading my Bible. It shocked me. I liked it, but I was shocked that I could do it and *enjoy* my time untainted with any sense of boredom or sleepiness.

Each morning, I would get up and go into my office and begin my devotions. Gail would get up and go into the living room. When we were done, we would get ready for the day. At the time, Gail was in school, so I was preparing to drop her off at school and go to the church. On the very first morning, as we sat down to eat breakfast together, Gail asked me a simple question: "What did you read about?"

She knew what I read about. We were reading the same sections of the book of Mark. I knew that what she was really asking was, "How did you apply that to your life?"

When I told her what I had journaled on, her response was simply, "That's interesting. I got something completely different out of that." This began a discussion that has continued for over thirty-three years now, and our kids joined the discussion. "What did you read about?" is still asked at our breakfast every morning.

Since that time, I have come up with a simple formula for personal devotions. Remember, I always asked, "How?" when people told me to have devotions. The focus of my ministry has been to help people answer that fundamental question and apply it in their lives. It is also the focus of the remainder of this book.

See, I believe that the meat of Christianity is not prophecy, last-day events, or any of the other fine details that churches like to talk about. First Corinthians says these are for the nonbeliever.[1] This is one reason we use prophecy seminars to reach people for Christ. These are not the meat of the Christian world but rather the milk. Many Christians get fixated on last-day events, while they never get to fully experience the gospel. You see, the real meat, once you've become a believer, is living and acting like a Christian.

The heartbeat of Christianity is finding a way to apply Scripture to your life. When I was learning to pray and journal through Scripture, I never prayed, "Lord, this is so important that Bob needs to hear it." Nor did I say, "I sure wish Gail would get this!" When Gail asked me in the morning, "What did you read about?" I never said, "I read what God wants you to do!"

Nope. The heartbeat of Scripture is how to apply it to *my* life, not to other people's. This is why I think that what happened next was so important.

---

1. To understand how to reach nonbelievers, take a look at my first book, *Evangelism Intelligence: Why Adventist Churches Grow Differently.* (You can find it on Amazon.)

THREE

YOU GOT A PROBLEM?

Most researchers agree that you form a habit in twenty-eight to thirty days. One brain specialist, Caroline Leaf, in her book *Switch On Your Brain,* says that you create a habit in thirty days, and you reinforce that created habit over the next thirty days (now a total of sixty days). Finally, you cement the new habit as a way of life over the next thirty days (now we are at ninety days). In other words, if you can make it through the first thirty days, you're doing great because you've gotten past the hardest part of the journey. Reinforcing that habit becomes much easier from day thirty-one to day sixty, and you make it very strong and hard to break as you practice the new habit from day sixty-one to day ninety.

I had created this habit with my personal devotions. I went through the thirty, sixty, and ninety days and beyond. It was a good habit that taught me many good things about Scripture and prayer. It was a habit that, just a few years earlier, I would have never thought possible to create in my life. The methodology we used, including the joint accountability to personal devotions with my wife, felt like a miracle in and of itself. But this was not to be the last miracle in my personal devotional life.

About three or four months into my devotional journey, I remember thinking one day, "Does this work? Am I going to be able to maintain this for the long haul? Will I burn out of this too? I know I've created a good habit after twenty-eight-plus days, but will it really change me?" Will this really work?"

I may have missed a day or two here or there, but now my devotional life was more on than off. I was amazed that my devotions were still going strong. I was reading daily. I was applying Scripture to my own life. I was enjoying my time with God's Word and prayer. I knew God was speaking to me. Yet, I still had to ask, "Does it work? Is it truly changing me for the better?"

Just asking the question made me begin to waver. I wasn't sure. The question itself discouraged me. I could not see any earth-shaking changes in my life. As far as I could see, I was still essentially the same person. I was consistently having devotions, but was it working?

Later that day, I was sitting in my car at a stoplight, minding my own business listening to the local Christian music station, and tapping my steering wheel as I listened. I was less than three blocks from home. As I sat there at the red light, I had no intention of ignoring the

I was reading daily. I was applying Scripture to my own life. I was enjoying my time with God's Word and prayer. I knew God was speaking to me. Yet, I still had to ask, "Does it work? Is it truly changing me for the better?"

"No Turn on Red" sign glaring at me. I was not in a hurry and wasn't crowding the intersection. I could wait for the light to change. I was peaceful and calm as I listened to the radio. I was literally just sitting and waiting.

It was at that undisturbed moment that my blissful world made a jarring change. A car went past me through the intersection. The lady in the car honked her horn with a long, loud blare that sounded like a sick sheep about to throw up. As she drove past, she waved at me with half of a peace sign—a.k.a., she gave me the finger!

My old instinct flared up! I was immediately angry and immediately outraged. I was not doing anything wrong. I was not out in the intersection. I was not rolling forward like I was coming into her path. I didn't even notice her until she waved at me as she went by. She came from a completely different direction, so I couldn't have done anything previously to her. As providence would have it, my light changed at that very moment. I turned and followed her. She turned into the next parking lot, and I pulled in behind her—literally. She found a parking spot, and I pulled up directly behind her, blocking any escape from my righteous anger that was about to explode! She had no right, no justification, and no business doing that to me. I never took well to people who flipped me off. My anger was in peak mode, and she didn't even know I was there. She was grabbing her purse and, I was sure, trying to put on a face that made her look like she was a decent, respectable person. I knew better.

I pulled in behind her and flung my door open, nearly

tearing it off the hinges. I always figured if you are going to be angry, do it with gusto! I grabbed the top of my door and pulled myself up to a standing position. I was about to walk up to her door and shout, "YOU GOT A PROBLEM?" (You do remember chapter 1, right?)

However, God hit me with His holy two-by-four that day as I stood there between my car and my open door. My devotions that morning had spoken to this very thing, and I heard a voice simply say to me, "What good will this do if you go and yell at her? You'll get mad, she'll get mad, and it will ruin your whole day. So? What good will that do?" I was stunned! It was clearly the Holy Spirit speaking at that moment. It was the clearest I ever heard God speaking to me. I do not know how long I stood there, but I am sure it was for just a moment or two. Then I climbed back into my car, put it in gear, and drove away. That lady never even knew that I followed her into that parking lot. I still do not know why she honked and gestured at me. But it did not matter anymore. God had just worked a miracle in my life.

As I drove the next two blocks to my home, tears welled up in my eyes, and all I could say was, "It works. It really works." I was overwhelmed with amazement that reading the Bible and praying was actually changing me. Sure, I gained some great sermon material as I studied the Bible more regularly. Sure, I could tell other people about the number of days I have been able to read my Bible and pray. Sure, I could say it was good for me.

This was different. This was life-changing.

No longer was this just a great morning routine, but it was affecting my thoughtless moments. This was affecting my immediate unconscious thoughts, my reactions. I was in awe of a God who could cut with His two-edged sword clear down to the core of my soul. I went home and journaled some more, giving thanks to God and praising Him for answering my questions about personal devotions so vividly. As long as I live, I will never forget that moment. It will always motivate me to keep going with my devotional life and my journey with Jesus.

My anger issues go way back. I remember once, as a kid getting a new squirt gun. My brother wanted to see it. This was a special squirt gun because it looked like it was straight out of *Star Trek*. My brother calmly asked to see it. I told him no. He, being the bigger brother, pressed the issue further, and I said no! We began to wrestle for the squirt gun, and I knew I was about to lose—he was bigger and stronger. However, I broke loose and ran off. He caught up with me, and then I knew I was going to lose. After all these years, I do not remember why I would not share with him and allow him to get his grubby hands on my brand-new squirt gun, but I am pretty sure it had to do with selfishness on my part. Finally, I broke away again. I threw the gun on the carpet and intentionally stomped my foot down—hard. The gun broke. *That will fix him; now, he cannot have it. Wait! Neither could I!* "Now, look what you did!" I screamed at his bewildered face. My anger had gotten the best of me. Uh-huh. That is the case with anger, right?

The book of James says, "Human anger does not produce the righteousness that God desires" (James 1:20, NIV). You know it's true. Living it out in my own life was never fun. Anger plainly does nothing good for us.

"Refrain from anger and turn from wrath;
do not fret—it leads only to evil" (Psalm 37:8, NIV).

"Do not be quickly provoked in your spirit,
for anger resides in the lap of fools" (Ecclesiastes 7:9, NIV).

"Anger is cruel and fury overwhelming,
but who can stand before jealousy?" (Proverbs 27:4, NIV).

When I say that my devotions were affecting my thoughtless moments, I am saying that normally, my anger got out of control very easily, but this time in the parking lot it did not get out of control. In fact, as my mind was fast approaching going beyond control, God reined me in with a simple thought—"What good will it do?" God was doing something mighty in me, and it had everything to do with Him. And I cried the rest of the way home that day in the car.

How can reading Scripture, an ancient book, change a person? How can something written some 2,000 years ago have any effect on anyone? We are about to discover the key pieces in the next few chapters. It's about more

Knowledge about the Bible is good. It is foundational. Yet, when building a house, you cannot stop at the foundation; you must build the whole thing. How many Christians are out there that know all about the Bible but fail to know the God of the Bible?

than head knowledge. It's about life application.

The life application is what was changing me. I was no longer simply reading the Bible. Now, I was reading it and applying what I read to my own life and seeing how it fit into my consciousness. In fact, I will go on record right now as saying that reading the Bible as simply head knowledge but not applying it to one's own life is almost pointless.

Do not mishear me, please. Knowledge about the Bible is good. It is foundational. Yet, when building a house, you cannot stop at the foundation; you must build the whole thing. How many Christians are out there that know all about the Bible but fail to know the God of the Bible? They know about the second coming of Jesus. They can tell you all the things wrong with their church. So many Christians know what the Bible says about the Sabbath, death, worship, hell, and more. Listen, though, to the words of Jesus, in Matthew 23. He said, "How terrible for you, teachers of the Law and Pharisees! You hypocrites! You are like whitewashed tombs, which look fine on the outside but are full of bones and decaying corpses on the inside. In the same way, on the outside you appear good to everybody, but inside you are full of hypocrisy and sins" (Matthew 23:27, 28, GNT).

How many Christians do you know who know much about the Bible? They know Bible prophecy, they know end-time timelines, and they know much Bible truth, but they do not really know God. They know *about* Jesus Christ, but they cannot really say they know Him. Listen

45

to me, please. Nothing will be better for you than to have a personal relationship with God. Absolutely nothing.

I was once accused of never preaching meat and only preaching soft messages. I asked the person what they meant by meat. This person meant I should be preaching prophecy—every week. They nearly demanded it. My response was something like this: My job as the pastor of this church is to give you a balanced diet. If all you ever ate was meat, you would die of a heart attack. However, what you are saying is that you want to stay on baby formula. You are going to starve to death. The real meat of Christianity is that you and I learn to live with Jesus as our best friend.

A columnist named Rod Dreher, writing about a totally different subject, but saying the same thing to his readers, quoted David Brooks: "Those men—and they seem to have all been men—must have listened to hundreds of hours of pious sermons, read hundreds of high-minded theological books, recited thousands of hours of prayer, and yet all those true teachings and good beliefs had no effect on their actual behavior."[1]

Dreher understands the basics of what I am talking about. Christianity must affect the day-to-day, or we are wasting our time. He again quotes Brooks: "How can there be such a chasm between what people 'believe' and what they do? Don't our beliefs matter? The fact is, moral behavior doesn't start with having the right beliefs."[2]

Is that you? Are you one of those people that can find scriptures and recite thirty-nine reasons why your friend is wrong on the grand theological themes of why certain musical styles are more holy than others? It does not have to be you. Keep reading. We are about to get to the meat.

---

1. David Brooks, "The Southern Baptist Sexual Abuse," quoted in Rod Dreher, "Southern Baptist Crash," The American Conservative, May 26, 2022, https://www.theamericanconservative.com/dreher/southern-baptist-crash/.
2. Brooks, "The Souther Baptist Sexual Abouse."

FOUR

DISCOVERING THE UNKNOWN PIECE

Dwight Nelson taught us what he taught university students about personal devotions. The key was to get them started—even if they only spent fifteen minutes a day—it would be better than not spending any time in the Word and praying. So, he taught us to start with the book of Mark, in a modern translation that is broken up into paragraphs. Then, he suggested that we read a paragraph a day and pray about what that scripture was saying to us.

In my journal, I would write down the key phrase or verse that really spoke to me at the top of the page. There is a good reason to do this. As we write Scripture, we are fulfilling the task of the Old Testament kings who were supposed to write daily parts of God's law. God directed that it was not to be done by a scribe but by the king himself (Deuteronomy 17:18–20). If the king followed the instruction, he could not easily walk away from God's words and commands. This daily writing of Scripture is part of a life change. It also helps in remembering what to say when you know your wife will soon ask you what you read about. In other words, reading is one part, and then writing is a memory tool.

I prefer doing my devotions on the computer, but I find I remember my devotions better if I do them by hand. Why? While I'm on the computer, cut-and-paste is so easy, but by hand, I must look at what I am copying/writing, and I must process it repeatedly while I write out the verse. I tend to utilize the computer more often, but when I do, I must take time to reread the passage and ponder it more slowly so that I remember and apply it.

Gail and I started reading the book of Mark, one paragraph at a time, as Pastor Nelson had suggested. Each morning I would come out of my office and she would come from the living room, and while sharing breakfast, we would begin by asking, "What did you read about today?" It was a new experiment for us, and we were both learning and growing. We were also very curious as to what was happening in each other's life. Most times, there was some surprise in finding that we could both read the same paragraph of Scripture and get something completely different out of it. We were surprised at the ability of Scripture to speak into our lives. It was as if we had never read those words before. This became a very enjoyable part of our journey, finding out what we had both seen in Scripture and how we were being challenged by it.

We were surprised at the ability of Scripture to speak into our lives. It was as if we had never read those words before. This became a very enjoyable part of our journey, finding out what we had both seen in Scripture and how we were being challenged by it.

Surprisingly, we found we were both falling in love with Scripture. Gail and I could not wait to get up and spend time with God. I remember spending an hour each day and thinking how incredible it was! Before this, I could not spend five minutes in prayer, and I didn't even try that often. Now, I was spending more time in God's word and wanting to spend more time talking to him than I felt I had time for. There was a sense of wonder, waiting to see what God would do next in our lives.

It was much later, many years in fact, that I found out what was making it stick and work for us. One word—*Accountability*. Accountability in the simple question, "What did you read and pray about today?"

There were days I wanted to get myself blissfully distracted in doing ministry or playing on my computer. I could have made phone calls, typed letters, written parts of my sermon, or just worked out in my office with the door shut. Yet, I knew that in the next hour or so, I would be sitting down to breakfast with my lovely wife, and she was going to say, "What did you read about today?" I also knew that I needed to have an answer or be sent back to start the day right!

We generally do not like the word *accountability*. We think of people being held accountable for their sins, their crimes, or for something that is not pleasant. We think of accountability partners, who seemingly lurk in the recesses of our lives to help us overcome some temptation, problem, or sin. However, in athletic pursuits, when my coaches held me accountable for practicing ball, running, or swimming, I knew it was a good thing. That kind of accountability that spurs us on to greater things is well worth it.

The Bible has this to say about accountability: "And let us consider how to stir up one another to love and good works, not neglecting to meet together, as is the habit of some, but encouraging one another, and all the more as you see the Day drawing near" (Hebrews 10:24).

Each time Gail and I sat at the breakfast table and asked, "What did you read about?" or "You gotta hear what I read about today! It was so cool!" we were spurring each other on to good works and encouraging each other on toward the coming kingdom.

This was the missing piece. Read, pray, *and then tell* someone else what you read about. When you tell someone something, it helps you remember it, and you integrate it into your life more and more each time you tell it.

You see, for years, as a kid, I had heard preachers tell me to read the Bible and to pray. I always wondered how. Adding this one piece to our personal devotions—telling someone else—is the missing piece that made it stick in my life. And it has worked for countless others.

Now, some thirty-three years later, we still do it. Even though our family has grown (we have eight kids), we still ask at breakfast time, "What did everybody read about this morning?" That kind of accountability is very important in the walk of faith. It's very important to continue to move us and shape us for the kingdom. It has helped shape our kids and helped develop within them a personal devotional life as well.

I do not know very many seven-, nine-, and twelve-year-olds that have personal devotions. I don't know very many teens that do, either. For that matter, I do not know many adults who do. However, this single accountability question added to a reading plan and a journal has trained my kids to make time for their devotions first.

What we did not know back then is that we had discovered the hidden piece that makes personal devotions "stick" in people's lives. Everyone hears that we should read our Bibles more and pray. Yet, *how to do it and keep it going* is the part that is often left out.

As a teenager, I remember sitting in church and listening to the pastor encouraging us to read our Bibles. I was a new Christian, and the only Bible experience I had was proof-texting. That is not a very satisfying devotional methodology. So, when the pastor would say, "We need to read our Bibles," or "You need to begin having your devotions," I would simply ask the fundamental question. How do you do that? As I stated earlier, I never received an adequate answer.

When Gail and I happened upon these three steps, we had no idea it would change so many people's lives. This three-step process of personal devotion has helped many people around the country in many churches.

When we tell someone what we are reading about, we accomplish several things. First, we are repeating it, making it less forgettable. We are very prone to forgetting things. Now, think with me. We read it. We wrote it.

Three Steps

1. Read the Bible, following a reading plan

2. Pray about what you read

3. Tell someone what you learned in your devotions

We journaled about it. Then we told someone about it. We make it more memorable and, therefore, more likely to change us during the day than a simple reading and silent prayer. Once in a while, I'll get up extra early, and by the time Gail asks me, "What did you read about today?" it has been three or four hours. During those hours, my mind has been focused on a hundred different items, and I cannot easily remember what I read about. Fortunately, I journal in an app called Evernote, and I can pull it up. Then the simple act of repeating it makes it more memorable. Rather than forgetting about it and going on about my day, I must recall it and repeat what I learned, and this, in turn, allows me to reapply it. It makes Scripture real *for me*.

The goal is not to read the Bible as a task on a checklist, a to-do item. It is not something to get done and then move on with the "important" things in life. It's also not about "Look how many days I had devotions this week/month/year" or about telling others how much of the Bible you read each year. No! *Knowing our Creator as our personal Savior, Lord, and God is the most important thing we will ever do.* The Bible is a relevant book that speaks to our current situations in life. We need to see it as such for ourselves. Remembering what we have read about and how it has been applied is absolutely necessary. The first thing we accomplish by repeating what we have read is embedding it firmly in our memory.

Secondly, we reinforce it for ourselves. Not only are we reading, but we're applying what we see there into our own lives. When I tell what I read, I am also telling what I see God saying to me. When I say it out loud, it becomes more readily applicable—I am remembering it, saying it, and re-hearing it!

Third, we are learning to share our faith and give a very simple yet powerful testimony. Can you imagine if you had a daily testimony and not one that is only about what you did in 1974, 1994, or 2014? In this way, we pass on the word of God to another person. Whenever we do that, we strengthen the body of Christ. At times I share my devotional thought on Facebook, Twitter, or email to friends, my family, and especially my wife. Currently, I blog about it on occasions when I think it might be helpful to my congregation or others. As we pass on the word to another, we are also helping them advance to the kingdom.

Additionally, a wonderful by-product of this is that it has strengthened my marriage. Each day, as Gail and I make sure that we have made God first, each other second, and ourselves last, it has grown our marriage in unimaginable ways. We have become travelers going in the same direction toward the same goal. We don't have time to stop and look at each other's warts. We are too busy enjoying the journey and getting closer to our destination.

Gail sees a very vulnerable part of me when I share what God is doing in me. I firmly believe that heartfelt praying with another individual is likely the most vulnerable and intimate thing anyone ever does. I think it is more intimate than sex. Why? It is more intimate because we share the very core of who we are. Most of the time, we keep some part of us distant from everyone else. We only share what we want them to know about us. Yet intimate, heartfelt prayer goes to the core, and when it is shared with another, unvarnished and unhindered, it is an intimacy that cannot be found any other way. Sharing with Gail like that, she has fallen deeper in love with me, and I with her.

For several years, Gail and I shared the entire written text of our journals via email with each other. Gail still does this with a group of ladies each day. Some of them do it via handwriting, so they simply take a picture of their journal entry and text/email it over to the other ladies. At one time, for about a year, there was a men's group in Cheyenne, Wyoming. We met at a coffee shop and sat around on couches. When we started it, I passed out *Life Journals*[1] and said, read one of the passages in the day's reading plan, journal your thoughts, and then let's go around and share what we've written. Most of the time,

Each day, as Gail and I make sure that we have made God first, each other second, and ourselves last, it has grown our marriage in unimaginable ways. We have become travelers going in the same direction toward the same goal.

the guys would read their entire entry. It was fascinating to see how we all grew and opened up to each other because of the simple hour-long study time in which at least half of it was spent all by ourselves with God, our Bibles, and our journals.

Read. Pray. *Tell.* That was the unknown piece that makes the changes we have been able to see in so many people's lives. Putting those simple steps into place is truly life-changing.

---

1. You may order the *Life Journal* from liferesources.cc.

FIVE

STRUGGLES

I do not want to give you the impression that everything went along without a hitch since that first morning of devotions. Hardly. If I said that, this book would be dishonest and hyper-pious of me. Plus, it would be useless to you because you will soon find out that it will not go that easily for you all the time, either.

I have come to believe that your personal devotional life is likely the most important thing you will ever learn to do. Because of its importance, the devil is going to hit you with everything he has. He simply does not want your devotional life to work. He does not want you to get close to God. He does not want you to find your way to God's kingdom. I believe the devil will do anything he can to get you to stop.

In the book of Daniel is a story of Daniel praying a prayer and the angel Gabriel taking twenty-one days to

I have come to believe that
your personal devotional life
is likely the most important
thing you will ever learn to
do. Because of its importance,
the devil is going to hit you
with everything he has.

come and answer it because the devil was trying to stop him. Maybe, three weeks is not that long, but we are talking about one of God's specially chosen prophets. Yet, here is an example of the devil seeking to do everything he can to stop us from getting connected to God and finding answers. Another example would be Jesus in Gethsemane.

A key theme in the great controversy between Christ and Satan is that Satan does not want you to experience God's wonderful, filling, life-changing love and grace. In fact, he does not want you to worship God at all! Therefore, to stop you, the devil will wake you up with indigestion, and you will not feel well enough to have your devotions. Your phone will ring, your email will ding, your kids will cry, your neighbor will need help, the power will go out, or any number of diversions. That online ad will finally be bringing buyers, your offer will be accepted, or your social media post will have hundreds of likes.

The issue here is this; the devil knows that this is the most important thing that you will do, so he will do everything he possibly can to get you to stop. If you can think of a few things that might interrupt you, know that the devil has perfected his abilities and has hundreds more ways to cause interruptions. On the other hand, think about this: "Our heavenly Father has a thousand ways to provide for us, of which we know nothing. Those who accept the one principle of making the service and honor of God supreme will find perplexities vanish, and a plain path before their feet."[1]

Here is an example of how things can happen: Gail and I had been going along well, sharing and growing for about a year and a half or so with our routine of devotions. Then our son was born. It was easy for me. When he cried, it was because he needed to eat, and I did not have the anatomical enhancements to do anything about that. Obviously, Gail loved our son and feeding him, but it caused a change of routine in her devotional life. She struggled because she had grown spiritually as much as I had and wanted to continue. God had done some amazing things in our lives, and we did not want to stop, but our son was waking up at 6:30 A.M. Gail began getting up at 5:30 A.M. so she could read and journal her prayers before he woke up. Then he began waking up at 6:00 A.M. Gail reluctantly set her alarm for 5:00 A.M. Slowly, this kept getting earlier and earlier until Gail was getting up at 4:00 A.M. just to make sure she was able to get to her devotions. She knew that once our son was awake, she would be tied up for the rest of the day.

However, 4:00 A.M. was just too much. She was becoming exhausted. We looked for solutions, and most of those revolved around trying to keep him asleep. None of them worked. It was also emotionally draining because nothing was the same, nothing worked, and we were losing ground on our devotional habits. Finally, we agreed that whoever got up first had their devotions uninterrupted while the other one got our son. Then after the first one finished, we would trade the boy and the Bible, and the other one of us got to have devotions. It worked well, and it was a solid agreement between us that helped hold us accountable. (We are not even going to talk about the unspoken race to be up first.)

This agreement worked perfectly. Our son was supported as a baby, we got the normal amount of sleep, and we both continued to grow in Scripture and prayer. This kind of fundamental adaptation is a necessary piece of personal devotion. You will sometimes have to flex. Some people do not like flex in their lives. Deal with it! Like I tell my kids, "Life isn't fair. Get used to it." Having the flexibility to support and help each other strengthened our marriage and our parenting, and we continued our journey down the path of spiritual growth.

It is simply inevitable that the attack of the devil will come, and we need to adjust to meet the trial or temptation. As James says, "Consider it pure joy, my brothers and sisters, whenever you face trials of many kinds, because you know that the testing of your faith produces perseverance. Let perseverance finish its work so that you may be mature and complete, not lacking anything" (James 1:2–4, NIV).

That is what we are looking for, right? To persevere in our Christian walk so that we will become mature, so God can finish His work in us and we will be complete, not lacking anything. That is what we want, so flex as needed.

I mostly do my devotions in front of my computer. I find I can type faster than I can write by hand. My typing does a better job of keeping up with my mind. At other times, I need the focus provided by using a paper Bible and paper journal to reinvigorate my devotional process. I periodically switch back and forth between formats just to keep myself thinking and open to what is happening.

In today's world, however, the only time I need to handwrite something is when signing the credit card machine at the store. It's a dying art. In fact, many schools no longer teach cursive handwriting. So, as mentioned earlier, I journal in an app called Evernote. Having it sync across devices in the cloud has saved me through many hard drive crashes and computer glitches. So, this is my go-to standard most of the time.

My wife has recently gone back to the paper Bible and journal, though. She likes the tactile feel and the distraction-free environment. Some of my friends use the Bible App or the YouVersion Bible App and pull up the *Life Journal* reading plan in that. It works slick and easy.

Doing your devotions in front of a computer or phone creates a problem, though. In front of my electronic device, I see all my to-do's, all my emails staring at me, or my family budget saying, "Deal with me first!" It is extraordinarily easy to get distracted. This, too, is a tool of the devil to keep us from our devotions. Email cannot come first. Phones ringing cannot come first. The family budget cannot come first. Yet, when we do our devotions online or on an electronic device, the distractions are very real and seem very pressing. I would be willing to bet that you are as distractible as I am, right? News, social media, email, texts, calendars, to-do lists, web surfing, projects, photos, and so much more. You understand what I mean.

So I have erected boundaries that my accountability partner (my wife) asks me about periodically. "What did you read about today?" is always the first question. The second question asks about priority, "Did you do it first?"

One of the biggest struggles we face is the life change that God puts us through. For some reason, we humans think we know a lot about stuff, and we think we should be in charge of our own lives.

Gail and I had a friend who was not a Christian. Her story can be summarized in just a few words: Pregnant, then married, in that order. Depression, suicidal thoughts, and divorce.

One day she opened one of our cupboards and found a Scripture promise taped to the inside of the cupboard door. She said to Gail, "Don't you ever take a break? Don't you ever take a vacation from that God stuff?" Gail simply said that since the devil does not take a break, we cannot either.

We had studied the Bible with her and her ex-husband. We had them over for dinners, parties, and play dates for our sons, who were the same age. We were friends. They had come to the evangelistic seminar we had. About a year after her divorce, she was talking with Gail about how a few mornings before, she woke up in a stranger's home, in bed with a man she did not remember ever meeting or seeing before, and she was in shock over what her life had become. As they talked, she said, "I don't trust God. I want to be in charge of my own life. I don't want anyone else in charge." Gail just looked at her and asked, "How's that going for you? No one can handle life on their own. We desperately need to let God be in charge."

In Job 38, God starts asking Job a series of questions: "Who are you to question my wisdom with your ignorant, empty words? Now stand up straight and answer the questions I ask you" (Job 38:2–3, GNT). What God is trying to show Job is that he does not know everything. He is trying to say there are things you must learn. God is simply saying, you can trust me, and you do not have to question everything that happens in your life. It is about continual conformity to God's character.

In the *Andrews Study Bible* notes for 2 Thessalonians 2:13–15, it says this: "A process of increasing, intentional conformity to the will and character of God by the power of the Holy Spirit."[2] The goal is to be walking in that direction continually. The aim is for the life to change, not stay the same. The miracle is in letting go of our anger, our lust, and our bitterness. It is the life change that we all long for, and it is truly a miracle when it happens.

Henry Blackaby, in his powerful workbook, *Experiencing God*, says that if God asks you to do something and your first answer is yes, then He is Lord of your life. "It is impossible to worship God and remain unchanged."[3] If you ever say no, then God is not Lord of your life. If God is going to be first, and if He is going to be Lord—in charge of—our lives, then you cannot say no to Him.

If Jesus is truly Lord, then we will do what He says, no matter what. That's what servants do. Anytime we

If Jesus is truly Lord, then
we will do what He says,
no matter what. That's what
servants do. Anytime we
say yes, He remains Lord.
As soon as we say no,
we have told the Lord that
we no longer want His
input on this issue, and we
have taken back lordship.

say yes, He remains Lord. As soon as we say no, we have told the Lord that we no longer want His input on this issue, and we have taken back lordship. We are now back in charge.

Taking back lordship isn't always about big things. Small decisions ultimately lead to bigger decisions. We must guard the avenues of our hearts and work toward saying yes, and never no, to God. Jesus said, "One who is faithful in a very little is also faithful in much, and one who is dishonest in a very little is also dishonest in much" (Luke 16:10).

We must learn to say yes to Jesus in the small and large things. They do not come easily. The reason they are so hard is because I like overseeing my life. I do not like submission. I am not good at letting God have total control. I have been around long enough to know that you probably do not do so well at it, either. How do I know? I have my wife's permission to share this story with you.

One day, I was up first and went to my office to have my devotions. I shut the door to make sure there was very little distraction. However, I heard that Gail and our baby boy were up soon after me, and she was entertaining him. But the sounds coming from the kitchen weren't totally happy.

When I finished, Gail gave our son to me, and she went into my office and closed the door. I played with him, got him some food, and in about an hour, Gail came out. I had already started to make our breakfast. Gail began to help.

There was something in the air, though. Tension. You know, when you can tell if someone is upset in the room? I could tell. I thought I had done something wrong, so I asked. Gail assured me I had done nothing wrong. But she was slamming . . . er, forcefully closing the cupboards, stomping around the kitchen, and generally not much fun to be around that morning.

I was about to tell her, "Why don't you go have some more quiet time." But before I could say that, she finally slammed yet another cupboard door and said, "Okay! I'll do it!"

"Do what?" I questioned.

She looked peaceful for the first time that morning as she said, "For the last couple of days, I have had the conviction that I should do something, and I didn't want to do it. Today that conviction was extremely strong right in front of me. I told God, 'No!' but He wouldn't let go of it. So, I finally said, 'Okay, God, I'll do it!' " Gail, in essence, was saying, "You are Lord, You know best, and You are in charge. I'm done fighting You."

That's surrender. It simply means we let God be in charge and be the Lord of our lives. And it is truly the hardest part of the spiritual life. It is about the changes that God wants to work in you and me. We all want to think we are doing pretty good. We all want to feel good about our lives. Some people are into change. Some are not. Yet, when it comes to making a life change in an area we really like (e.g., food, music, entertainment, friends, etc.), we tend to buck hard when pushed to change.

When you really invest in your personal devotional life, you will begin to see what changes are needed. Usually, those changes are not where you want to make them. They do not always come at the most opportune time for you. They are usually things you would rather not notice and just wish God would leave you alone instead!

Yet, the miracle of life change is ever marching forward. And the joy of following God and doing life His way becomes so amazing that you will never want to go back on it. We are always much better off listening to God. For me, I'm not going back. Although I have my struggles, I would rather have Him as Lord of my life than have me back in that role. My goal is to live up to the new creation that I am (2 Corinthians 5:17). Who in their right mind would want to keep the old life?

---

1. Ellen G. White, *The Desire of Ages* (Mountain View, CA: Pacific Press®, 1940), 330.

2. Jon L. Dybdahl, ed., *Andrews Study Bible* Notes (Berrien Springs, MI: Andrews University Press, 2010), 1577.

3. Henry Blackaby, *Experiencing God* (Nashville: B&H, 2006), 3.

SIX

OVER TIME

Over time, our house became a house of prayer. But it was not an easy journey. When we first discovered this great asset to our spiritual walk, I wanted to tell my congregation that they could grow too. Yet, each time I preached about personal prayer, my prayer life would do a swan dive off the deep end and finish in a massive belly flop into an empty pool of non-spirituality. Each time I would preach about personal devotions, my devotions would lag, and it was a struggle to get it going again.

It was as if God and I were walking on a spiritual high, but as soon as I began to speak about what He was doing in my life, seeking to encourage others, I would trip and fall off my routine. I was not up in front bragging. I simply wanted to share my testimony and help others along their own spiritual journeys. But when I did, the devil came and kicked my chair out from underneath me.

I remember all too well that my personal spiritual life would be going on pretty well but then would drop off in the low times. Just when I needed it most, it was like I had nothing to hold on to. In other words, my spiritual habits worked, except in the low and discouraging times when I would struggle along without them.

Eventually, I determined I would never preach about my personal spiritual life again. It was too costly. It was too hard to get going again. My prayer life was *that* important to me. If I sacrificed my own spiritual life to help others, the cost would be too high. I was growing, changing, and God was working miracles in my life. I never wanted to lose that again. I am not saying that was a good reaction; rather, I was simply seeking some self-protection for my spiritual life.

There were other times that my devotions went along well until times got hard—a problem in life, a discouraging feeling in my soul, or troubles at work. These all seemed to be attacks of the devil on my personal spirituality as well. I remember all too well that my personal spiritual life would be going on pretty well but then would drop off in the low times. Just when I needed it most, it was like I had nothing to hold on to. In other words, my spiritual habits worked, except in the low and discouraging times when I would struggle along without them. Yet, it is the low times when we need spiritual strength most, right? I mean, the low times are when you need God to carry you, not abandon you. This is what the old poem about footprints in the sand was talking about, right?[1] I knew I had to keep my devotional practices going.

If you are going through a divorce, a bankruptcy, a job firing, or are seeing your kids going through an incredibly lousy time of life, you need God *then*, right? If your work projects are behind, you cannot seem to catch up with email, or you are sick with the flu or cancer, *that* is when you need God there with you, not just in the good, stable times.

So what was going on? Something different needed to happen. When I most needed God, my devotional life would tank. It shouldn't be that way.

I cannot say exactly what happened that changed it. I can only surmise that it was the good and healthy habit of doing devotions every day. Simply getting into a good habit made the difference. When you do something every day for years, you begin to create a strong habit that, at some point, cannot be broken. This is a vitally important piece of personal devotion. We will be talking about this in a later chapter.

One day I said to Gail, "I feel more down and discouraged than ever, but this is the first time I've been able to stay with my devotions during the lows." It was not the most striking set of readings or the greatest prayer time of all. Yet, what was remarkable was that during this particular low time, I was able to continue going forward with my daily devotions. I was not gaining new ground, but I was not slipping backward, either. That is when I knew my devotional life had passed another milestone. The first milestone happened when I began reading the Bible and praying daily. The second milestone happened when I was able to keep going, even through the low times.

This was actually quite a breakthrough. For years, I never had a devotional life. Then just when it got started, it would stop because I was discouraged about something at work, angry at my kids, or in some other troubling situation. During the low times, devotions usually stopped. I cannot tell you what actually happened to change things for me. I can only attribute it to the routine and habit of the daily ritual. That just made it—finally—easier to stay on track with my devotions.

The third major milestone happened when others began to follow suit with us. They took a cue from us and learned what we had been doing. They began copying us, learning and growing too.

Here's what happened:

My wife was friends with a couple of ladies who were dealing with some really big issues—past abuse, divorce, and some other really ugly things. Gail told them about the three steps of prayer we had learned: (1) read, (2) pray, and (3) tell. You cannot even begin to imagine the horribleness done to these two ladies. The stories were intense, and the ladies carried a lot of baggage because of their past. They wanted help. So, when they would call and begin to cry, complain, or ponder new ideas about their problems, Gail would stop them and bluntly ask, "Have you had your devotions and prayer time yet?" Gail wasn't being trite. She just knew this was beyond her, but not beyond God. She thought if they could surrender this to God and learn to trust Him first, then she could step in, add her support, and help them.

Turns out, neither of them knew how to consistently read and pray to start the day. With small kids in the home, finding a quiet space was next to impossible. Gail found out about it and told them to bring their kids over to our house. She would watch the kids while each lady individually went into my office and had some quiet time.

Gail knew that the best counselor they could have was Jesus. She did not have all the wisdom in the world, but she knew Jesus did. Gail would watch the kids, or they would find someone else to watch them, and they would individually come and have quiet prayer time, seeking to find where God was leading.

The first time I knew about it, I came home to find one of their cars out front. When I came into the house, the owner of the car was nowhere to be found. Gail was inside cooking dinner. I came in, said hello, and headed to my usually empty home office. Gail grabbed my shirt and said, "You can't go in there!"

I was a bit dumbfounded and asked, "How come?"

"Something big is going on in there. It sounds like a baby is being born, but it's probably a new life in Jesus that is taking root."

At that point, I was really confused. But then I heard this moaning, sobbing, and groaning coming from under my office door, and I thought, *Is there really someone having a baby in there?* Gail kindly explained to me that she had lent my office to someone who needed private space.

This actually went on for about a year. I never knew if I was going to be able to utilize my home office or not. I soon learned to take anything I thought I might need when I left, or I might not get it back for several hours when I needed it. But despite that, I was glad. These

I had an instructor in college who used to say, "You do not really understand something until you can explain it to someone else." I have found that especially true in the spiritual realm. It is hard, but when you can tell someone else what has happened and how to reproduce it, you have come a long way.

ladies were learning to work through their deep pain with Jesus. They were learning how to go to Him when they could not go anywhere else.

When they came out of my office, they would sit and talk with Gail about what happened. Gail was not counseling. She was simply listening to them tell what they had prayed about and what they had learned from Jesus. Gail was helping them by holding them accountable for their personal spiritual growth. And that was helping to make it stick in the process.

I had an instructor in college who used to say, "You do not really understand something until you can explain it to someone else." I have found that especially true in the spiritual realm. It is hard, but when you can tell someone else what has happened and how to reproduce it, you have come a long way.

That is what takes place in a person's devotions when they explain what they have learned in the Bible and how it has affected them personally through the life application process. It changes a person from the inside out.

---

1. Mary Stevenson, "Footprints in the Sand" (1936), https://footprints-inthe-sand.com/index.php?page=Poem/Poem.php

SEVEN

SAME OLD, SAME OLD

I am the kind of guy who gets bored pretty easily. Remember when I said that I had that new Bible and wrote some thoughts in the margin of Proverbs? I was on fire the first day. I loved the second day. By the third day, the last day I ever did it, I was pretty ho-hum. I am the guy that wants new food, new restaurants, new clothes, new whatever. I like new. New songs, new preachers, new members, anything but the same old, same old.

So, I started my devotional journey in Mark. When I finished Mark, I pondered where to go and decided on Philippians. From Philippians, I went to Ephesians. Then I traveled to John. When I got done with that, I meandered around some and found myself back in Philippians. Then into Ephesians again. I limited myself to the parts of the Bible that looked interesting, and some of the Bible clearly did not sound interesting. I repeated

I realized that I had maintained

my steadiness in having

personal devotions, but I

was utilizing others' personal

growth to show where mine

should go. I began to feel

a lack again—like I needed

more. I needed the Bible.

some books and never made it to others. Soon, I drifted into reading religious/spiritual books in the morning that utilized Scripture. I read *The Desire of Ages* and *The Great Controversy*, both by Ellen G. White. Then I went to a couple of Chuck Swindoll books, then onto some others by a famous preacher or two. The material was always of a spiritual nature, but it was mostly someone else's thought process. It was good, but it was not the best thing for my full spiritual growth.

Ultimately, I realized that I had maintained my steadiness in having personal devotions, but I was utilizing others' personal growth to show where mine should go. I began to feel a lack again—like I needed more. I needed the Bible. But the Bible was getting harder and harder to read. It didn't have all the fun stories. It was older and not as much fun or interesting to me. I realized I would rather read a book about the Bible than read the Bible itself.

It reminded me of a cartoon I had seen years before. People were flocking to books for $25 that talked about the Bible, but there were stacks of Bibles for sale at 50 percent off, and nobody was buying them. Seems backward, right?

At the time, I was pastoring in Colorado, where we had been church-planting. At a conference of church planters, I happened to win a trip to Hawaii to spend a week with a large growing church. The pastor was Wayne Cordeiro. I had never been to a conference of this size before. (There were only thirty senior pastors there, and I was the only Seventh-day Adventist.) And I had never been to a conference where they spent the first day and a half dealing with the pastor's personal spiritual life.

I was shocked for two reasons. First, many of those senior pastors were saying to me and others, "He's probably right; I really should have some personal devotional time." Whoa! How in the world can you lead a congregation spiritually if you aren't growing yourself? I am not trying to judge anyone here, but please understand the demands that are placed upon a pastor. Pastors carry a lot of stress about other people's lives, visitation, running the church, finances, growing the church, demands of new members, and demands of the organization, and they do it 24/7/365. It can really wear emotionally on a pastor. I simply could not understand how those pastors could continue to deal with the stress and care of their members if they were not finding the time and place to feed themselves.

You see, even though I was not in the Bible, I was still having devotions in other spiritual books. I had already learned that my best stress relief was when I was in prayer. I had found that when things were getting out of hand, I could go and spend time in prayer, talking it out with God. I worked through my own mistakes, my addictions, the stress of members' failed marriages, and the stress of friends who were in crisis. I would not have survived if I did not have Jesus to lean on. There was simply no way.

At the convention, Wayne Cordeiro took what Dwight Nelson had told us and added some additional steps that

I believe are crucial to our personal spiritual growth. We had already learned these:

1. Read the Bible
2. Pray (journaling your prayers)
3. Tell someone about it (What Gail and I discovered by accident on our own)

Pastor Cordeiro added some steps to the list for clarity, support, and help.

4. Have a reading plan (He put together the *Life Journal* reading plan that helps you read through the Old Testament once and the New Testament twice in the same year.) A reading plan allows you to have a place to go when you are not sure where to read next. The plan simply answers that question for you. It also keeps you from coming back to the same areas while ignoring other areas of Scripture.
5. Bring your calendar and to-do list to your devotions. Why? So that while you are reading or journaling and a thought comes to you—write it down—so you can move right back into your devotions without missing a beat. If you do not write it down, you will do one of two things. Stop your devotions and deal with that so you will not forget it, or you'll just keep playing it over and over in your head, not really focusing on what God is seeking to tell you.

Pastor Cordeiro's *Life Journaling* concept is fairly straightforward, and I have found its format to be helpful for my own personal journaling. The daily devotions are built around the acronym SOAP—Scripture, Observation, application, and prayer.

Scripture. The Scripture plan is to read about four to five chapters a day. Pick one verse, one section, or one idea that stands out to you and write that in your journal. I am often struck, after doing this for eighteen years now, that I see things in Scripture that I "never saw before." It is quite amazing, actually, how readings of Scripture line up with current events in my own life.

Observation. The observation section is for taking the scripture again, and in your journal, write down what's going on. "Just before this passage, the disciples were headed . . ." Or "The Pharisees were trying to trap Jesus here when they asked him this question." You are observing the text—taking into context what is going on before and after it. I often take a look at commentaries in this section also. The key is to observe the context, the teaching, the outcomes, why it was being told, or anything else you see.

Application. The application section is about applying what you read to your own life. This is not a time where you say, "This is a great section for my son." Nope. This is about taking a scripture and asking yourself questions. It is seeking God's answer to how the passage applies to our own life.

For me, I've concluded that this is the *key* to spiritual growth and truly walking with Jesus on a daily basis.

Head knowledge of Scripture is useful to a point, but if it's not life-changing, we really do not have a testimony to share, and we are not being changed daily by the word. Applying Scripture goes way beyond head knowledge. It is about life change.

Prayer. Prayer is simply that. I journal my prayers just like Pastor Nelson taught in that camp meeting talk so many years ago. I journal my prayers because it keeps me on track and because we are told, "We have nothing to fear for the future except as we shall forget the way the Lord has led us, and His teaching in our past history."[1]

I used to journal in WordPerfect, then in Microsoft Word. But after experiencing lost floppy disks, lost hard drives, and computer crashes, I now journal in the Evernote app. I can then take my journal entries with me on my phone, my tablet, my computer, or anywhere and they are not subject to computer crashes. I often use my devotional ideas for the various worship talks I give at schools, board meetings, staff meetings, or other places I am called upon to share a message.

Here in the remainder of this chapter are some quoted examples of my personal prayer journey:

May 25, 2019—Wealth and Destruction
Scripture: "Now the weight of gold that came to Solomon in one year was 666 talents of gold" (1 Kings 10:14).

Every year King Solomon received over twenty-five tons of gold, in addition to the taxes paid by the traders and merchants. The kings of Arabia and the governors of the Israelite districts also brought him silver and gold. Solomon made two hundred large shields, each of which was covered with about fifteen pounds of beaten gold, and three hundred smaller shields, each covered with about eight pounds of beaten gold. He had them all placed in the Hall of the Forest of Lebanon.

The king also had a large throne made. Part of it was covered with ivory and the rest of it was covered with pure gold. Six steps led up to the throne, and there was a footstool attached to it, covered with gold. There were arms on each side of the throne, and the figure of a lion stood at each side. Twelve figures of lions were on the steps, one at either end of each step. No throne like this had ever existed in any other kingdom.

All of King Solomon's drinking cups were made of gold, and all the utensils in the Hall of the Forest of Lebanon were of pure gold. Silver was not considered valuable in Solomon's day. He had a fleet of ocean-going ships sailing with King Hiram's fleet. Every three years his fleet would return, bringing gold, silver, ivory, apes, and monkeys.

King Solomon was richer and wiser than any other king in the world. They all consulted him,

The application section is about applying what you read to your own life. This is not a time where you say, "This is a great section for my son." Nope. This is about taking a scripture and asking yourself questions. It is seeking God's answer to how the passage applies to our own life.

to hear the wisdom that God had given him. Each of them brought Solomon gifts—articles of silver and gold, robes, weapons, spices, horses, and mules. This continued year after year.

King Solomon also had four thousand stalls for his chariots and horses, and had twelve thousand cavalry horses. Some of them he kept in Jerusalem and the rest he stationed in various other cities. He was supreme ruler of all the kings in the territory from the Euphrates River to Philistia and the Egyptian border. During his reign silver was as common in Jerusalem as stone, and cedar was as plentiful as ordinary sycamore in the foothills of Judah. Solomon imported horses from Musri and from every other country (2 Chronicles 9:13–28, GNT).

Solomon loved many foreign women. Besides the daughter of the king of Egypt he married Hittite women and women from Moab, Ammon, Edom, and Sidon. He married them even though the LORD had commanded the Israelites not to intermarry with these people, because they would cause the Israelites to give their loyalty to other gods. Solomon married seven hundred princesses and also had three hundred concubines. They made him turn away from God, and by the time he was old they had led him into the worship of foreign gods. He

was not faithful to the LORD his God, as his
father David had been (1 Kings 11:1–4, GNT).

Observation

Ever since I first read this, and saw the *only* other time
in Scripture (and 2 Chronicles 9) outside of Revelation
and the mark of the beast, the number 666, I saw a deep-
seated connection between this and the mark of the beast.

The rest of the passage shows the opulence of how
Solomon lived. It shows that he broke basically *all* of
God's three laws for the kings—stacking up gold, adding
wives, and adding chariots. The opulence and wealth
in which he lived just set him more and more against
God.

Application

I have to stop and wonder if the whole 666 thing in
Revelation isn't more closely tied to wealth and gold than
anything else. The other main time in Revelation that gold
is mentioned is when it talks of paving streets with it.

I have to wonder about America, founded on godly ideals
and principles, and how they have walked completely away.
This includes all Western society, at least, but it's spreading
farther than just Western society. Could it be that our
wealth has made us careless? Could it be that our wealth
has made us ungodly? Could it be that we trust more in
our money than we trust in anything godly?

So I also have to wonder about my personal finances.
Yes, I've been focused a lot on finances lately, trying to

get them figured out to make them all happen correctly. Yet, it could cause unforeseen problems by taking away my focus from other important things.

Also, the statements I've made recently reflect the idea of retiring now and moving someone where cheap and just living out life in a way that isn't as stressed on ministry, and so forth. Could it be that the devil would like to get us out of ministry? Could it be that our financial picture could get in the way of our work for God? May it never be!

Prayer

Spending time in prayer.

* * * * *

May 16, 2022—Retributive Judgment

Scripture: He who dwells in the shelter of the Most High will abide in the shadow of the Almighty" (Psalm 91:1)

> For he will deliver you from the snare of the fowler
>   and from the deadly pestilence.
> He will cover you with his pinions,
>   and under his wings you will find refuge;
>   his faithfulness is a shield and buckler.
> You will not fear the terror of the night,
>   nor the arrow that flies by day,
> nor the pestilence that stalks in darkness,

nor the destruction that wastes at noonday.
A thousand may fall at your side,
    ten thousand at your right hand,
    but it will not come near you.
You will only look with your eyes
    And see the recompense of the wicked (verses 3–8).

Abstain from every form of evil.
    Now may the God of peace himself sanctify you completely, and may your whole spirit and soul and body be kept blameless at the coming of our Lord Jesus Christ. He who calls you is faithful; he will surely do it (1 Thessalonians 5:22–24).

Observation

We just had a discussion about Psalm 91 the other day. My question in the family was, how do you know if you can apply this to you or not? I got accused of not believing in Scripture and not being able to trust anything if I didn't apply the principles of the promises to myself. My question isn't about God's ability. My question isn't about the prophecies. My question is, how can I apply the promises of God that were spoken to a specific person at a specific time to me?

This verse may provide an interpretative key: the various threats of life listed in the poem can be understood as punishments (reward) for the wicked; it does not mean general disasters or natural calamities, but God's judgments on the evildoers. Consequently, a calamity may strike a believer (see the case of Job), but the believer is free of God's punishment or retribution for evil because he stays in the Almighty (verse 8; see Exodus 15:26).[2]

Application

This partially answers it. Number one, it's a poem. It's meant to be uplifting, powerful statements and not necessarily meant to be divine facts. Secondly, it's talking more about the promise of what will happen to the evildoers than it is about the righteous. It's basically saying that the evildoers will experience all these things, but God's people will not receive God's punishments. It's not talking in general about the stuff we all face, death, destruction, sickness, etc. But a believer will not have this happen because of God's retributive judgment.

I believe that.

Prayer

Lord, lead me to the foot of the cross daily so that I might live in obedience to You in all that I do and in all my ways.

* * * * *

December 14, 2019, 4:32 A.M.—Let Us Run to Jesus!
Scripture: Hebrews 13:11–16 (GNT)

The Jewish high priest brings the blood of the animals into the Most Holy Place to offer it as a sacrifice for sins; but the bodies of the animals are burned outside the camp. For this reason Jesus also died outside the city, in order to purify the people from sin with his own blood. Let us, then, go to him outside the camp and share his shame. For there is no permanent city for us here on earth; we are looking for the city which is to come. Let us, then, always offer praise to God as our sacrifice through Jesus, which is the offering presented by lips that confess him as Lord. Do not forget to do good and to help one another, because these are the sacrifices that please God.

Observation

The bodies of the sacrificial animals are burned outside the camp. Jesus was destroyed outside the camp. We don't have a permanent home here. So, let's run to Jesus. That is our permanent home. That is our structure. That is our base.

I like the imagery of running to Jesus. He's outside the city. Don't go to Him. Don't walk to Him. Don't meander to Him. Don't go anywhere else. Run to Jesus.

I also like the imagery that we do not have a permanent city here for us. The city was a wall of protection. It was

I like the imagery

of running to Jesus.

He's outside the city.

Don't go to Him.

Don't walk to Him.

Don't meander to Him.

Don't go anywhere else.

Run to Jesus.

safety. But with no permanent city, it says, don't settle. Don't get too comfortable. You won't be staying long. Don't sit and wonder what you can do next to make it yours. No, we don't have a permanent city/home/house here. We are waiting for something much better.

> "Lift up your tired hands, then, and strengthen your trembling knees! Keep walking on straight paths, so that the lame foot may not be disabled, but instead be healed" (Hebrews 12:12, 13, GNT).

That's when this passage seems to come into play. Keep going straight. Lift up your hands, strengthen your knees, and walk to Jesus for healing.

> As for us, we have this large crowd of witnesses round us. So then, let us rid ourselves of everything that gets in the way, and of the sin which holds on to us so tightly, and let us run with determination the race that lies before us. Let us keep our eyes fixed on Jesus, on whom our faith depends from beginning to end. He did not give up because of the cross! On the contrary, because of the joy that was waiting for him, he thought nothing of the disgrace of dying on the cross, and he is now seated at the right side of God's throne.
> Think of what he went through; how he put up with so much hatred from sinners! So do

not let yourselves become discouraged and give
up. For in your struggle against sin you have
not yet had to resist to the point of being killed
(Hebrews 12:1–4, GNT).

Again, then this passage seems to give us comfort and
courage. Many have gone before us and made it. We can
too. Keep your eyes fixed on Jesus. That's where everything depends. Don't get bogged down in the vines in
front of you. Keep your vision on Jesus. Don't worry
about how tough you may have it right now. Jesus went
through so much more. He clearly did a lot more. You
aren't suffering and dying yet.

Run to Jesus. He's the permanent home you have.

Application

Those are good words for me. Don't get bogged down
by [people]. This is nothing like what Jesus faced. Rather,
stay in tune with God, and keep your eyes on Jesus. He
went through so much more. Because of that, he can carry
you through anything else. Besides, this isn't your permanent place. That may mean our home, it may mean the
church, it may mean whatever. Don't get your hopes in
the here and now, today, keep your eyes focused on Jesus.

---

1. Ellen G. White, *Testimonies to Ministers and Gospel Workers* (Mountain
View, CA: Pacific Press®, 1944), 31.

2. Jon L. Dybdahl, ed., *Andrews Study Bible* Notes (Berrien Springs, MI:
Andrews University Press, 2010), 745.

EIGHT

THE GOOD-ENOUGH CONTINUUM

What really is the point of making morning devotions a habit? Is it a checklist item that you can check off daily so that you can brag to your friends about how much you read that day or how many days you have read the Bible? Nope. Is the point of it to get through the whole Bible in a year? Although that is pretty cool, that is not the goal.

The real goal is that when you and I actually embrace the Word of God daily, it changes us. When we learn to dig into God's Word every morning (or evening) and apply it to our lives, it becomes all-encompassing, and it shapes us. When, after thoughtfully reading it, I apply it to my own life circumstances, I learn more and more of what the Bible means, and it grows me in my obedience and surrender to God.

If it is true that God speaks to us through Scripture,

I am profoundly changed
when I apply Scripture to my life.
It starts with asking a
simple question each day,
"How will my life be different
today because of what I read?"
Addressing Bible study through
this question is life-changing.

and He does, and if it is also true that I need to learn to live in accordance with Scripture, and I do, then these come together when I make time to read Scripture and apply it through life journaling. I am profoundly changed when I apply Scripture to my life.

It starts with asking a simple question each day, "How will my life be different today because of what I read?"[1] Addressing Bible study through this question is life-changing. It puts the whole of Scripture in my pocket, teaching me how to walk daily with Jesus. Instead of Scripture just being a bunch of random stories about people who made dumb or wise decisions, instead of being about deep theology and commentaries, instead of being about strange prophecies, it now becomes a place for me to see how and where God is leading me. Scripture begins to make sense, and shapes my life to become more like Christ's.

The Bible is still the most-sold book in America today. The average home in America has three to five Bibles in it. Yet, nobody is reading the Bible. George Barna recently reported that 51 percent of Americans believe they live by a biblical worldview, yet only 6 percent of them actually do.[2] If we are not reading the Bible, it cannot shape our worldview at all. I have heard it said many times, if we ate one meal a week, we would soon starve to death. Spiritually speaking, we must learn to feed ourselves and not rely upon someone else's teachings about the Bible.

Christlikeness is the goal. I am not arguing for perfection. I am arguing for the idea that you and I get on a journey with Christ and walk with Him every day. To explain the process, I would like to provide some theology. What I'm about to express first is not good theology, but bear with me a moment, because I believe we all suffer from this bad theology from time to time.

Imagine a continuum where every person is placed along a line running from very bad to very good. We'll call it the "good-enough continuum." On one end of infinity, we see God. On the other end, we see the devil.

DEVIL ⟵――――――――――――⟶ **GOD**

On this continuum, we'll place various people where we imagine they belong. We put Billy Graham, Mother Teresa, Ellen G. White, John Wesley, and other great Christians way off to the right, closest to God. They are very close to God—almost there.

DEVIL ⟵――――――――――――⟶ **GOD**

On the left end of the continuum, we place people like Hitler, Ted Bundy, Genghis Khan, Hell's Angels, and other truly evil people. They aren't quite as bad as the devil, but almost.

DEVIL ⟵――――――――――――⟶ **GOD**

Now, in the middle of this line, there is the cross. We tend to think that anyone to the right of the cross is saved, and anyone to the left of the cross is lost.

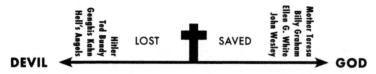

Many of us tend to put ourselves just barely left of the cross because we don't feel good enough, or we place ourselves just to the right of the cross because we know we aren't *that* good.

Now, here's the point: This whole concept is based on bad theology. The fact is you and I cannot be good enough to get to heaven. We will never produce enough good works to get us to heaven. We will never be able to earn our way to heaven. "For the wrath of God is revealed from heaven against all ungodliness and unrighteousness of men, who by their unrighteousness suppress the truth" (Romans 1:18). "All have sinned and fall short of the glory of God" (Romans 3:23).

All have sinned. This means that even Billy Graham, Mother Teresa, Ellen G. White, and all the others are lost without Christ. No matter where they are on the good-enough continuum, they are *not good enough* to get to heaven. It does not matter if they are better Christians than you. It does not matter if they lived a better life than you. They are all sinners and therefore are subject to God's wrath. However, there is a way out.

"All have sinned and fall short of the glory of God, and are justified by his grace as a gift, through the redemption that is in Christ Jesus" (Romans 3:23, 24). "The wages of sin is death, but the free gift of God is eternal life in Christ Jesus our Lord" (Romans 6:23).

This free gift of God is provided by way of Jesus Christ. He is our only path to God and heaven. "For the Scripture says, 'Everyone who believes in him will not be put to shame.' For there is no distinction between Jew and Greek; for the same Lord is Lord of all, bestowing his riches on all who call on him. For 'everyone who calls on the name of the Lord will be saved.' " (Romans 10:11–13).

If all have sinned, and if all deserve death, and if we cannot be good enough to get to heaven, then what hope is there?

Imagine with me for a moment that there is someone on our continuum that has always been faithful to his wife, never abused a child, always returned a faithful tithe, never cheats on his taxes, and is an elder in the church. In our bad theology, we would put this person far up the line to the right.

DEVIL ←—————————————→ GOD

Christianity is not about
evaluating how good
we are. It is only about
walking with Jesus in the
same direction and daily
experiencing His free
gift of salvation.

Now we will take another imaginary person. He has gone down the whole sex, drugs, and rock-and-roll path of the world. He is in prison for murder. He is a pretty bad dude. In our bad theology, we would put this guy far down to the left.

Now comes the reality. What if the good guy on the right says to God, "I don't want to follow you down this path any longer." He does not start cheating or stealing, or anything else. He is still a "good guy," but suddenly, he is walking in the wrong direction.

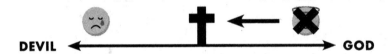

Now, suppose the guy on the left says, "God be merciful to me, a sinner. I can't do this anymore. Would you take control?" He still has a lot of really rough edges, but he is now walking in the right direction.

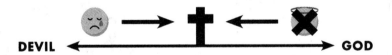

So, which one is following God?

See? *The whole concept of a "good-enough continuum" is false!* The guy on the left is, in reality, closer to God.

Why? Salvation has never been about how good you are. It has never been about being good enough. What really matters is the direction you and I are walking.

We are wrong in even placing ourselves or someone else anywhere along the line. Christianity is not about evaluating how good we are. It is only about walking with Jesus in the same direction and daily experiencing His free gift of salvation. Jesus illustrated this in the parable of the Pharisee and the tax collector.

> Two men went up into the temple to pray, one a Pharisee and the other a tax collector. The Pharisee, standing by himself, prayed thus: 'God, I thank you that I am not like other men, extortioners, unjust, adulterers, or even like this tax collector. I fast twice a week; I give tithes of all that I get.' But the tax collector, standing far off, would not even lift up his eyes to heaven, but beat his breast, saying, 'God, be merciful to me, a sinner!' I tell you, this man went down to his house justified, rather than the other. For everyone who exalts himself will be humbled, but the one who humbles himself will be exalted (Luke 18:10–14).

Jesus is simply saying the same thing here—what matters is the direction you are walking. One of the men considered himself saintly and didn't need any help from God. He was holier than everyone else, and that was all

The journaling method I'm describing in this book is designed through its life application process to get us walking in the direction of Jesus. That is the only thing that really matters. That is where the rubber meets the road, so to speak.

that mattered to him. The other, the tax collector, knew he was not holy. He had been taught that by the Pharisees. Everywhere he turned, the people put him down and kept him from understanding his true station in life. He was not holier than *anyone* else. He was most certainly a sinner. Jesus then comes back at the end and says it doesn't matter one whit about your station in life. Your present status does not matter. Your past does not matter. What matters is the direction you are walking. That is all.

Certainly, in Jesus' parable, he's teaching several things about the Pharisees and the stupidity of their view of God and other people. But the main thing, I think, for purposes of our discussion here, is that Jesus says it doesn't matter where you are on the good-enough continuum. What matters is which direction you are walking.

The journaling method I'm describing in this book is designed through its life application process to get us walking in the direction of Jesus. That is the only thing that really matters. That is where the rubber meets the road, so to speak. Establishing the proper devotional habits brings us into a closer walk with God every day because it forces us to apply Scripture to our personal life. This is not about some nitpicking theological argument with your Uncle Bob, nor about arguing in some online forum about the theological aspects of a particular author's writing. This plan is about reading for your own growth, your own understanding, and your own application.

You can certainly study the theology of the Bible as you

go. And you will certainly catch things that make a good argument to your Uncle Bob. Yes, you will undoubtedly do all of that. But *the purpose* is to ask how it will affect you personally and your walk with God today.

---

1. This question appears at the bottom of each page of the *Life Journal*.

2. George Barna, "Perceptions About Biblical Worldview and Its Application," Center for Biblical Worldview Family Research Council, https://downloads.frc.org/EF/EF21E41.pdf.

NINE

DANIEL

Daniel was one of those Bible people that had great faith. He is one of very few that the Bible says absolutely nothing negative about. That could be because he wrote the book about himself, or it could be because he had great faith in God. I choose to believe that it was because of his faith.

Most people know the story of Daniel and the lions in chapter six. The story progresses to a remarkable point: Daniel disobeys a law so that he can continue praying to God. "When Daniel knew that the document had been signed, he went to his house where he had windows in his upper chamber open toward Jerusalem. He got down on his knees three times a day and prayed and gave thanks before his God, as he had done previously" (Daniel 6:10).

There are several things of particular interest in this verse. First, he was disobedient to the law of the state.

Second, he prayed three times a day. Finally, he had a habit of praying every day already. I want to focus specifically on the third aspect—the habitual part of Daniel's prayer life.

Daniel had formed this habit over years and years. It was the core of his life. It was the reason he could stand up before Nebuchadnezzar decades earlier and tell him that he was going to go crazy (Daniel 4). In Daniel 2, we have a record of Daniel spending time in the evening asking God to reveal King Nebuchadnezzar's dream to him so he could give its interpretation. In Daniel 1, we have a story of a young man full of integrity, and he was going to do what was right no matter the outcome. Daniel had developed a habit of turning to God for answers, wisdom, and guidance.

Some people view the idea of habitual personal prayer time and personal devotions as a bad thing. They say that your devotions should come from the heart and not be something habitual that doesn't even make you think. However, habits are simply what we do all the time. Habits are whatever is normal for us. The nice thing about having a habit of doing devotions is that when you do not feel like doing your devotions—and that day will come—you can fall back on your habit and do it anyway.

For me, there have been many times I have not felt like having my devotions. Listen, when I stay up late at night, getting up in time for my devotions is hard. When I'm not feeling well, when I'm stressed, when I'm in a rush, when my email pings or a text from my kid comes in, I have a hard time sticking with my devotions.

In Daniel 1, we have a story of a young man full of integrity, and he was going to do what was right no matter the outcome. Daniel had developed a habit of turning to God for answers, wisdom, and guidance.

Worse than the interruptions, though, are the dry times we all experience. Not every day of my personal devotional life is a mountaintop experience. Just this morning, before writing this, my devotions were thought-provoking but not super exciting or wonderful.

That is the beauty of forming a spiritual habit. It's not dependent on how I feel. That's also the beauty of accountability. Part of the reason I was able to form a habit in my personal devotions is because I knew, in the morning at breakfast, my wife was going to ask a simple question, "What did you read about this morning?" Interestingly, this didn't start out about accountability but about genuine curiosity as we both began to discover the habit of personal devotion. However, as it turned out, it helped us develop a habit that protects our time with God even when we don't feel like it.

Habits and accountability go hand in hand. Although it isn't the only way to form good habits, I do recommend you find someone to go down this journey of personal devotion with you. This goes back to the chapter about the three steps: read, pray, and tell someone. It helps make the Bible stick with you.

The best part about making a spiritual habit out of your devotions is that when you do not feel like it, you get up and say, "I don't feel like having my devotions this morning." But what do you do? You get up and have devotions anyway.

This morning my reading plan dealt with the story of Pilate at the trial of Jesus. I was impressed with two things as I read. First, listen to your wife! It will save you a lot of heartache later. Second, I was impressed with the idea that Pilate did not have the moral integrity to say no to the Jews about crucifying Jesus even though he knew that Jesus was not guilty.

This is where we come back to the story of Daniel. The reason Daniel could stand up to the immoral laws of his boss, his king, and his friend was that he had developed moral integrity through his daily time with God. Daniel was unwavering in his experience with God precisely because of the pattern built into his life.

We have all heard the stories of communist China and how they persecute Christians on a regular basis. People are sent to hard labor work camps for nothing more than owning a Bible. Similar stories came out of communist Russia in times past and other places as well. Yet, when the communist revolution took over in China, and the Christian missionaries were thrown out of the country, the church merely went underground. The fascinating thing is how fast and how large the underground church grew.

How did it grow? How did people have the courage to withstand beatings, imprisonment, and punishment for their faith? The same way Daniel had. "When Daniel knew that the document had been signed, he went to his house where he had windows in his upper chamber open toward Jerusalem. He got down on his knees three times a day and prayed and gave thanks before his God, *as he had done previously*" (Daniel 6:10; emphasis added).

The reason Daniel was a hero is precisely *because* God was able to use him for amazing service *because* Daniel made himself available to God every day. Every. Single. Day. Without fail. Even when unpopular and hard.

This book has been written as a simple challenge to begin the daily habit of having personal devotions. If you don't have them now, Daniel's challenge of three times a day is tough to imagine. Yet, what if you began with simply fifteen minutes a day in the mornings? What if at noon you took time to pray a little more than "bless this food"? And what if at night you prayed with your kids?

The challenge isn't about how many times a day you have prayer time. The challenge isn't about how long you spend in prayer. The challenge is simply to pray and begin the regular habit of praying and applying Scripture to your life. That's why I like this method so much. I have seen that answering one simple question after reading the Bible has changed many lives. "How will your life be different because of what you've read today?"

The reason Daniel was a hero was not because he survived lions and ate only vegetables. And not because he could interpret dreams. Daniel was a hero precisely *because* God was able to use him for amazing service *because* Daniel made himself available to God every day. Every. Single. Day. Without fail. Even when doing so was unpopular and hard.

It is like we tell our kids, "Do the right thing, even when it's hard." That is the message I see in Daniel, and it's why I dare to be a Daniel and to fight Satan's band.

TEN

AS EASY AS A WORKOUT

When I learned to journal my prayers and follow a reading plan, I tried and tried to teach it to people and to my congregation. However, it wasn't until I learned about the *Life Journal* plan from Wayne Cordeiro that I really had the tools to teach it to my congregations.

I took those tools back to my congregation in Colorado and began to teach the methods to them. When I started, roughly 25 percent of the congregation reported having daily personal devotions. I preached a couple of sermons on the topics I'm sharing with you in this book. We handed out journals as much as we could. Initially, we gave everyone a journal, but every year we would hand out the reading plan again. I preached about personal devotions every December with the intention that people would get the new year started well.

When I left the congregation in Colorado, we took an

actual survey that showed us the number of those who were having regular, daily devotions had grown from 25 percent to 65 percent. I believe this was a win!

No man can of himself understand his errors. "The heart is deceitful above all things, and desperately wicked; who can know it?" Jeremiah 17:9 (KJV). The lips may express a poverty of soul that the heart does not acknowledge. While speaking to God of poverty of spirit, the heart may be swelling with the conceit of its own superior humility and exalted righteousness. In one way only can a true knowledge of self be obtained. We must behold Christ. It is ignorance of Him that makes men so uplifted in their own righteousness. When we contemplate His purity and excellence, we shall see our own weakness and poverty and defects as they really are. We shall see ourselves lost and hopeless, clad in garments of self-righteousness, like every other sinner. We shall see that if we are ever saved, it will not be through our own goodness, but through God's infinite grace.

But no man can empty himself of self. We can only consent for Christ to accomplish the work. Then the language of the soul will be, Lord, take my heart; for I cannot give it. It is Thy property. Keep it pure, for I cannot keep it for Thee. Save me in spite of myself, my weak, unchristlike self.

> Mold me, fashion me, raise me into a pure and holy atmosphere, where the rich current of Thy love can flow through my soul.[1]

A good friend of mine described it this way in an email to me. This came about a year after my first sermon series on the devotional plan. Here is what he said:

> This is based on a journal entry of mine from a couple of months ago. I think it applies to the topic of personal study and journaling that you are doing in December. If you think it is helpful, feel free to use it (no names, please). If not, no prob.
>
> Last month, I decided that I was going to get in shape. It's a long story about how I came to that decision, but it involved years of neglect of my health, eating whatever I wanted, sleeping only when necessary, and avoiding exercise as much as possible. "That's it," I said to myself one day, "I can't stand looking at you anymore, and we are going to do something about it." So, early the next morning, I dragged out some old running clothes, sucked in my gut in order to get the shorts on, stuffed my feet into running shoes, left my wife sleeping blissfully, and treadmilled my way through twenty-five tortuous minutes of great pain, rivers of sweat, and profound questioning of my own sanity. After

carefully considering whether the dull ache in my side was an early sign of a heart attack (I'm pretty sure it wasn't) and deciding that calling 911 was not necessary, I made my way back into the bathroom to start getting ready for work. As I passed by the mirror, I did what all guys do: I checked myself out to see what a manly man I was! Amazingly enough, I found myself disappointed that I wasn't looking better already! Apparently, I expected that one early morning workout was somehow going to counteract years of early morning Krispy Kremes, lunch-time cheeseburgers, and an incredible attraction to late-night Doritos! I was really upset! "*This isn't working!*" I thought. I was ready to quit on the spot. Thankfully, I didn't, and today, one month later, the exercise is easier, the sweat is less profuse, and the pain is virtually gone. The guy in the mirror still isn't eighteen, but he has gradually gotten a bit less offensive!

I am struck by how similar this process has been to spending time in the morning every day, studying the Bible, journaling, and praying. When I first started doing that, to be honest, it was painful! I'm not a morning person, and I'd much rather sleep than get up to read the Bible. More to the point, though, when I did manage to get up for quiet time, I found myself disappointed that I didn't change right away!

"I mean, come on! I read the Bible this morning! How come I just said that horrible thing to my kids? Why do I still struggle with my temper? *This isn't working!*" What I know now is that it takes time. It took me a lot of years to make myself a spiritual mess, and a few mornings with Jesus doesn't take all those old habits, thoughts, and flaws away instantly. He has promised that when I seek Him, I will find Him, but He doesn't say it will take five seconds. I believe that knowing Jesus is a journey, one that is well worth it and one that is life-changing, but I also know that if you give up on it too soon, you will miss an amazing journey. I haven't gotten rid of all my messes and flaws yet, by any means, but with His help, I guess I find myself "a bit less offensive" now!

That's what daily time with God does. It changes us. It doesn't change us immediately. We did not become spiritual messes in one day, so just as it took time to become a mess, it'll take time to replace that mess with godliness. In fact, God told the Israelites the same thing when he was bringing them into the Promised Land. As they were preparing to go into the land, God promised to take care of their enemies with hornets, but then he proceeded to tell them how *they* were to do it. *I will do it for you,* and here's how *you will do it*! In other words, God is saying, "I will work with you to get it done."

We did not become spiritual

messes in one day, so just as

it took time to become a mess,

it'll take time to replace that

mess with godliness.

This is what He actually said to them: "The LORD your God will clear away these nations before you little by little. You may not make an end of them at once, lest the wild beasts grow too numerous for you" (Deuteronomy 7:22).

God says, I will do it, and here's how you will make it happen! It is the same way with personal devotions and life change. It does not happen immediately or all at once. We are in the process of growth, and that takes time. We need the struggles to make us stronger. It is almost as if God says, you will not learn enough if I drive out your character flaws all at once. You would not be able to deal with the success if that happened.

You did not build a twenty-year addiction to pornography in a month. It is going to take time with God to experience a sustainable victory with Him. You did not develop your present struggles with food, anger, impatience, or selfishness in one day. Between you and God, it will take some time to obtain sustainable victory.

What do I mean by sustainable victory? Mark Twain supposedly said, "Quitting smoking is easy. I've done it hundreds of times." That is not a sustainable victory. When I say sustainable, I mean the victory that lasts and is with you for the rest of your life. It means never going back to that sin in your life again.

One pastor friend of mine took this concept home to his congregation. He taught it to his accountability partner, the school principal. That principal told me years later, "The *Life Journal* saved my life!" As I understood him, he was lost spiritually and dying spiritually daily. The time spent with God began to change him and gave him the power to lead his school with God at the helm rather than him. Today, that principal continues to utilize these concepts of daily devotion and continues to lead a godly school because of it. I know because he's my school principal now.

I have been using the concepts of the prayer journal now for about thirty-three years. I have been using the actual *Life Journal* every year for the last eighteen years. Every year, I read the same Bible passages on the same day of the year. I have a friend who has continued to use it daily for nineteen years.

I have another friend who, when he learned about it from me, decided to buy a nice journal and make his entries clean and nice and give it as a gift to his daughter so that, in time, his daughter could benefit from the spiritual journey of her father. Another friend took the reading plan and reduced it to a single page so that he could more easily carry it with him. We still hand it out every year at Christmas to my congregation. I have inserted the reading plan into my LOGOS Bible Software program, so each day's reading is simply a click away. Another friend found the reading plan on the website BibleGateway.com. It is also available on www.bible.com and the YouVersion Bible app that many people have on their phones. God has made His word readily available today, more than ever before.

Occasionally my kids will say to me, "Dad, you need

There is a vast amount of knowledge and understanding in Scripture that so many of us miss on a day-to-day basis. The Bible is the only book I know that I can read every year, day after day, for eighteen years, and still say, "Wow! I've never seen that before!"

to get a real Bible." My response is, "Oh, you mean a papyrus scroll?" What is a real Bible anyway? Is it only bound up in a faux-leather cover with gilded edges in traditional paper book format? Or is Scripture the words that were written down? My opinion is if you can read from your phone or computer, then by all means, do so. However, I encourage you to shut off your notifications while you do it, or you may never make it through the sea of distractions.

There is a vast amount of knowledge and understanding in Scripture that so many of us miss on a day-to-day basis. The Bible is the only book I know that I can read every year, day after day, for eighteen years, and still say, "Wow! I've never seen that before!" You cannot get tired of reading Scripture. It is a book full of knowledge that God wants to reveal to us on a regular basis when we are ready to listen and surrender to Him.

I have a church member who told me a delightful story some time back. She telecommutes for her work in a medical office. The doctor and staff are Christian and have weekly devotional time for the members of the office who want to join. Once or twice a year, my member travels several hours to the office for a week of work on-site. It was her turn to give the devotions. Here is what she told them:

"Every year in December, my pastor preaches about the same thing. Do you know what it is?" There were guesses, including Christmas, Jesus, and various other things. She assured them they were not likely to guess, so she told them I preach each year about personal devotions. She then went on to tell them all about the system of reading, journaling, etc. Mostly she shared a journal entry or two with them and told how it had transformed her life and her Christian experience.

After the devotional, one lady in the office asked if she could have the information about personal devotions that had been shared. She related how her Christian life was wavering, and she needed to get back on track. Later that day, another person came to my church member and asked for the material. Then after she had gone home, she got a couple of emails asking for the materials.

There is a great need in the hearts of people to connect with God. It has been called a God-shaped hole. Only God can fill that hole. People are longing for that.

Years ago, my wife was attending the Pacific Northwest College of Art in Portland, Oregon, as a student. After the Thanksgiving break, she noticed that one particular guy, Casey, was not back at school. So did everyone else, and the students began to talk about it. Somehow, word got back to the students that Casey had committed suicide over the break.

Gail felt like we should go visit the family. So, we found Casey's address, made a gift basket of fruit, and went to make the difficult visit to the family.

As we talked to Casey's mom, she described what happened and how sad she was, of course. But then she said something I will never forget. "Maybe Casey found what we are all searching for. Maybe this was his escape to a better reality. Maybe Casey found what he was looking for."

My head began to spin, and in my mind, I thought, *No! Casey died because he could not find what he was looking for! Casey did not find it, and that is why he committed suicide!*

I was reeling on the inside. On the outside, we gave the lady a hug, said a prayer, and told her if she needed anything, to please call.

It saddens me to see how many people are looking for God in all the wrong places and calling it all kinds of things. It saddens me to know that if they would simply look, they could find what they are looking for.

It is not just secular, non-Christians who are searching for meaning and direction. Not at all. Many Christians are troubled and searching for meaning and something better. We only find it in Jesus, through the Bible and being filled with the Holy Spirit. We only find it as we become absorbed in God's Word, listen to Him, and apply it to our lives.

Scripture, observation, application, prayer. It's life-changing. I've personally seen Scripture change two whole churches—hundreds of people, and most of all, me and my family. It can do the same for you if you are willing to give it a try.

In the introduction, I gave a link where you can order the *Life Journal*. There are many resources to teach you more and a variety of different journals. However, you can simply use a one-dollar notebook. I encourage you to get started. The goal is to get into God's word. I change translations every year just for variety's sake. This keeps me from glossing over and getting used to the words. When I read it in a different translation, it helps me see something different. So, every January, I change the default translation in my Bible software.

Please let me know how it goes for you. You can send me an email at coachenator@gmail.com and let me know if it is working for you. I believe it will.

---

1. Ellen G. White, *Christ's Object Lessons* (Review and Herald®, Washington DC: 1941), 159.